The Dynamite Animal Hall of Fame

by Bruce Weber

A Dynamite Book from Scholastic Book Services

The Book You Are Holding Is 100% Dynamite!

Yes, Dynamite Books come to you from the same scintillating scribblers and peerless pen and inkers who bring you *Dynamite* magazine every month: Jane Stine, Editorial Director; Wozney & Lucik Design, Art Direction; Sharon Graham, Production Editor; Susan Hood, Assistant Editor, plus the whole Hot Stuff gang!

Cover/Tom Leigh

Lots of humans helped put this book together. Several deserve special attention. Peerless and tireless Annette Weber took time out from raising our children to put in countless hours with book and pen. And the staffs of both the Paramus (NJ) Public Library and the Paramus (NJ) High School Library contributed mightily — B.W.

No part of this publication may be reproduced in whole or in part, or stored in a retrieval system, or transmitted in any form or by any means, electronic, mechanical, photocopying, recording, or otherwise, without written permission of the publisher. For information regarding permission, write to Scholastic Book Services, 50 West 44th Street, New York, N.Y. 10036.

Copyright © 1979 by Scholastic Magazines, Inc. All rights reserved. Published by Scholastic Book Services, a division of Scholastic Magazines, Inc.

12 11 10 9 8 7 6 5 4 3 2 1   5   9/7 0 1 2 3 4/8

Handy Guide to What's Inside

Let's Open the Door

Animals come in all sizes and shapes. There are friendly animals and not-so-friendly ones. There are quiet animals and some very noisy ones. There are some animals you'd love to have around the house; there are others that Mom wouldn't allow within 10 miles of home.

Our animal friends can make us laugh and cry — and most of all, they can make us love them.

Your particular favorite may be the kind who likes to lie around and not do much. You won't find him (or her) in *The Dynamite Animal Hall of Fame*. What you'll find here are the all-time amazings: the stars of stage, screen, and television; the heroes of war and peace; the record-breakers; and, of course, a few weirdos.

Inside *The Animal Hall of Fame* you'll meet Benji, Lassie, Morris, and the rest of the TV stars. You'll also find out about dogs that help blind people, deaf people, and police people. You'll meet some special animal people — those wonderful folks who've dedicated their lives to working with animals.

Most of all, *The Dynamite Animal Hall of Fame* is fun. It's one place where you won't find any signs reading "Beware of Dog." Here, they're the stars. Enjoy!

That's Show Biz

Step right up! It's our first stop, the Animal "Show Biz" Hall of Fame. Here you'll find all of your favorites — the animals that make you laugh, or cry, or cheer, or maybe all of the above. Stars of radio (you remember radio!), TV, movies, Broadway — they're all here, waiting for you.

HOLLYWOOD'S BEST FRIEND

The most famous dog ever? It has to be Lassie. Star of seven movies and a long-running television series, Lassie still spells M-O-N-E-Y at the box office.

The role of Lassie — there actually have been six Lassies — was "born" in 1943. Metro-Goldwyn-Mayer was making a movie called *Lassie, Come Home*. Its human star was Elizabeth Taylor.

"We need a collie," said the man from MGM.

"I've got one," said dog trainer Rudd Weatherwax. "His name is Pal."

"Sorry, Rudd," said the MGM talent scout. "The part calls for a female dog, Lassie."

The story might have ended there. But it didn't. The film was shot during the summer. That's when female collies shed their coats. It happened to MGM's female collie. The studio came running back to Weatherwax.

"Can Pal take a screen test?" they asked.

"You bet," he answered.

And so Pal, the male collie, became Lassie, the female star. He was a natural actor. Whether he was swimming, running, barking, or doing anything else he was asked to do, Lassie was a pro.

That's how Pal started the Lassie tradition. He went on to star in six more movies. Then his son (and four more generations) took over. They made it big in television. In fact, the *Lassie* TV series, which began in 1954, ran for 19 years. It was one of the longest-running TV series of all time.

How does a tradition get started? In Lassie's case, almost by accident. Rudd Weatherwax and his brother owned a pet obedience school. One day, a man brought in an eight-month-old collie named Pal.

"He barks all the time," complained his owner.

The Weatherwax brothers went to work and cured Pal of his bad habit. By that time, the owner decided he didn't want the dog anymore. Rudd was happy to keep him and was able to make him a star.

The family of Lassies always gets first-class treatment. They deserve it. Today's Lassie, the star of the 1978 film *The Magic of Lassie*, is the great-great-great granddaughter of Lassie I. When she works on a film, she lives in her own air-conditioned van, complete with bed, dishes, Lassie-monogrammed towels, shampoos, and a dryer. She has her own hairdresser, of course. And she has her own foot — er, paw — specialist.

Off the movie set, Lassie lives with trainer Weatherwax in Zuma Beach, California. She

has plenty of company. There are six other dogs, including her father and son. The others are a German shepherd, a Yorkshire terrier, and a pair of silky terriers. There are also a couple of horses, eight cats, 200 pigeons, and a host of other animals. They're all at the ready, of course, for the next Lassie movie or TV show.

On the road, Lassie is treated just like any famous star. When she was in New York in 1978, publicizing her movie, she stayed at the famous Plaza Hotel. Her meals came from — where else? — room service. If this is a dog's life, it isn't bad!

BOW-WOW — WOW!

During the 1920's and 30's, many Americans found it hard to make a dollar. Meanwhile, one actor in Hollywood was earning $1,500 a week — plus a share of every picture he made.

What did the star do with his money? For one thing, he bought a lot of dog food.

The star was Rin-Tin-Tin. From silent movies to TV, he was one of the greats. Rinty, as his fans called him, made 40 full-length movies. Many of them were written by Darryl F. Zanuck, who became one of Hollywood's most famous producers.

Rin-Tin-Tin was a German shepherd. Where did he come from? One story has it that he was found wandering on a battlefield during World War I. The German soldiers, so the tale was told, had left him there.

Rinty's owner and trainer, Lee Duncan, had another story. He said the dog found *him* in Hollywood and followed him home!

Either way, Rinty was a great star. He wasn't just a great dog that was well-trained. Rin-Tin-Tin was an actor. Like any great actor, he kept getting better and better. In the early days, you'd see Rinty looking straight into the camera, waiting for his instructions. In his later films, the dog just seemed to know what to do. It was uncanny.

As Rinty developed as an actor, the writers gave him more to do. His early pictures were all action. The later ones gave the dog a chance to act. It was scary. This German shepherd would look right at you and make you laugh or cry or even pray. And he did it all with his face!

In one picture, *The Night Cry*, Rinty successfully battled (and killed) a vulture on the edge of a cliff. In another, *Where the North Begins*, he was suspected of killing a baby. So he turned detective and found the culprit.

Rin-Tin-Tin was so successful that he made his studio, Warner Brothers, rich. They could take chances on other movies because they knew that Rinty's money was in the bag.

There were other dog stars: Peter the Great, Napoleon Bonaparte, Strongheart, even one called Dynamite. But none of them were in Rinty's class.

The German shepherd, who lived in his own five-room house, was as great a star as any of the humans he worked with — and probably smarter than some of them, too!

INSTANT REPLAY

If Rin-Tin-Tin could be a superstar, why not Won-Ton-Ton? That's what the folks at Paramount figured a couple of years ago. So they made *Won-Ton-Ton, The Dog That Saved Hollywood.* Wonty(?) didn't save Hollywood. In fact, he didn't even do much for Paramount.

But it did make a nice living for a nice German shepherd named Gus (who played Won-Ton-Ton). And it gave an entertaining couple of hours to movie fans everywhere.

Did Gus get special treatment when he became a star? He got to ride in a Cadillac and wear a diamond collar. But according to his owner, Karl Miller, that's it.

"He wanted to sleep in my bed," says Miller. "But that's where I drew the line."

In the movie, Won-Ton-Ton had to lick the face of actor Ron Leibman. "I put chopped liver on my ears to encourage him," reports Leibman. "Gus finished the liver, then started on my ears." Result: three dog bites for Leibman.

FOR THE LOVE (AND MONEY)

If you love famous dogs, chances are your favorite these days is Benji. Everyone wants a piece of the cuddly little mutt who starred in *Benji* and *For the Love of Benji*.

That's great for Frank Inn, Benji's trainer. The 350-pound Inn has been training all kinds of show biz animals for more than 40 years. But he never had one like Benji before.

Benji's story starts like so many others. Trainer Inn found Benji in a Burbank, California, animal pound in 1968. He named him Roscoe and put him to work on TV, as the pet dog on *Petticoat Junction*.

The sandy-haired pooch was just what the folks down at the Junction wanted. They did 39 shows a year. Roscoe managed to work up 39 different stunts. That went on for seven years. Everyone made money.

When it was over, Roscoe was old and tired. Frank Inn gave him what he deserved — a peaceful retirement. It didn't last.

A man in Texas wanted to make a movie about a dog. He had a good idea. He wanted to make the whole movie from the dog's point of view. He had a story, money — everything except a star.

Enter Frank Inn and Roscoe. The man from Texas, Joe Camp, visited Inn's animal farm. Frank and his wife have nearly 500 animals on hand. Most of them are dogs. Camp checked them all — but couldn't find the one he wanted.

Then he spotted Roscoe. "That's him," said Camp. "That's the dog I've been looking for."

"Forget him," said Frank Inn. "He's great, but he's too old."

Camp insisted. Old Roscoe became Benji. The rest is history. The first movie, *Benji*, took in nearly $50 million. Roscoe-Benji turned out to be a great actor, just like Lassie and Rin-Tin-Tin before him. It was great.

Joe Camp wanted to make another movie, *For the Love of Benji*. The original dog was too old

and sick. So they needed a replacement. Frank Inn tried to come up with a Benji look-alike. It took awhile, but he finally found what he was looking for. The only dfference: Benji II was (and is) a girl. Nobody has ever questioned it.

Number two was just as popular. She (he) lives in Frank Inn's house, sleeps in his bed, and eats steak and ice cream at his dinner table. "Why not?" says Inn. "She works for it."

That's for sure. Outside of her movies and TV specials, Benji makes personal appearances — for $7,500 each.

Thanks to the Benji "industry," Frank Inn

doesn't work much anymore. But he's not ready to give up on a good thing. While Benji II is earning her daily bread, Benji III — another look-alike — is waiting in the wings.

Joe Camp, the man who invented Benji, is thrilled. "Benji II is a better actor than Benji I," he says. "No matter what we ask the dog to do, it gets done. Sometimes it gets done perfectly the first time. We're not always that lucky with our human actors."

LUCKY DOG

Cats, so the story says, have nine lives. They don't, of course. But Sandy, the dog star of the Broadway musical hit *Annie*, seems to have had at least that many.

Before making the comic-strip dog come to life on stage, the floppy-eared Sandy was (1) abandoned several times, (2) almost put to sleep in a pound, and (3) nearly killed by a truck.

But Sandy survived all those near-misses to steal the show — and "write" his own life story in a book.

Sandy had a variety of homes in New York and Connecticut before landing up in a pound near Hartford, Connecticut. The day before Sandy was scheduled to be destroyed, he was rescued by 19-year-old Bill Berloni. Berloni, part-time actor and part-time carpenter, was asked to find and train a dog for the Sandy role in *Annie*. It cost him eight bucks. But eight dollars was never better spent.

Sandy was an instant smash. In rehearsals he was super. But two weeks before opening night, trouble struck again. Sandy was resting under a truck to avoid the hot summer sun. When the truck started, Sandy was hurt badly. He dislocated both legs and tore some muscles. He was nearly killed — again. But, like a real show-biz trouper, Sandy — and the show — went on.

Like a ballplayer, Sandy isn't always perfect. He has his off-nights and slumps. From time to time, he has: (1) blown his cues, (2) fallen asleep on stage, (3) skipped part of his role, and (4) taken time to scratch himself during a big song-and-dance number.

The human actors in *Annie* are good. But none is as popular as Sandy. His "paw-tographs" are always in demand. He signs them by inking his paw with a stamp pad, then pressing his paw onto paper. Imagine what his dressing room floor looks like.

"You never know what he's going to do on stage," says Berloni. "He may or may not bark when he's supposed to. He may stand around, staring at the balcony. You never know."

Does Sandy like being in the big time? He sure does. He eats steaks at some of New York's best restaurants. He has met two presidents — Gerald Ford and Jimmy Carter — and a host of other famous people. He has his own taxi that takes him to the theater every day. Not a bad life.

At the Tony theater awards show, owner-trainer Berloni showed up in a tuxedo. So did Sandy! What a lucky dog!

THE FINICKY MILLIONAIRE

Everyone loves Morris the Cat. Even if you don't like cats, you have to love Morris.

That's what makes the folks who make Nine Lives cat food happy. Morris, you see, sells cat food.

Was Morris always that lovable? Not really. When his trainer found him, he was only minutes away from death at a local pound. Morris was just another stray around Chicago.

His trainer saw something special in Morris. "He just looked like a cat who had seen the wrong side of life. He was just scruffy enough. I knew he could make it."

Morris sure did. He made the great commercials for Nine Lives and he starred with Burt Reynolds in the movie *Shamus*. He also won a Patsy Award, the highest award an animal can win.

In his heyday, Morris kept a lot of other people at work. He had a secretary to answer his letters. A public relations director kept him in the news. And there were security people to keep Morris from getting clawed by his fans. Of course, Morris had his own veterinarian. Every star should have his own doctor!

Cat-lovers everywhere mourned for Morris the Cat. He's gone now.

But there's hope for a new star. Her name is Tiger Raz. Her owners, the Fred Raz family of Portland, Oregon, found her in a trash can. But when a cat-food company looked for the cat with the best meow, Tiger beat out half a million other cats. Her prize: $15,000 and a trip to Hollywood.

Now Tiger is in TV commercials and she could become the next famous finicky feline.

BACK IN THE SADDLE AGAIN

The movie cowboys and their horses went — practically — hand-in-foreleg. One of the most famous was Champion, who belonged to the singing cowboy, Gene Autry.

Champion was a beautiful chestnut-colored horse. In fact, there were three horses called Champion. Each was a Tennessee walking horse. And each was born on the same farm in Tennessee.

Autry made even more money on records than in the movies. His fans demanded to see him, and he flew around the world to keep them happy. Champion always went with him.

Crowds everywhere cheered man and horse.

Interestingly, the first Champion had originally belonged to another cowboy star, Tom Mix. Tom called him Tony.

But the stallion's real name was Lindy. Why? He was born the same day Charles "Lindy" Lindbergh landed in Paris on his famous solo flight across the Atlantic.

Every cowboy had his special horse. Ken Maynard, for instance, had Tarzan. The Lone Ranger had his horse, Silver. His Indian companion, Tonto, rode on Scout.

But Gene Autry's Champion was special. There was an unwritten rule in western movies. You couldn't see the hero kissing the girl. At the end of most Autry movies, Gene would move in on the female star. The camera immediately switched to Champion, who would watch the whole scene with shock. When you heard the kiss off-camera, Champion would become disgusted.

Then, when the camera cut back to Gene, he'd be wiping the lipstick away. That always made Champion — though not necessarily Gene — happy!

QUICK ON THE TRIGGER

One of the most famous movie cowboys is still famous today — as a fast-food salesman. That's Roy Rogers, who with wife Dale Evans entertained millions.

Everywhere that Roy went, you were bound to

find Trigger, his famous palomino horse. (Dale's horse was called Buttermilk.)

During World War II, many movies were dedicated to a "Win the War" effort. One of the great film scenes of the period showed Roy and Trigger chasing after a runaway jet rocket that belonged to the Germans. Incredible!

Even after the horse's death, Roy and Trigger are still together — Rogers had Trigger stuffed and mounted. You can see him at the Roy Rogers Museum in Victorville, California. You can see Buttermilk there too.

Incidentally, TV and the movies must have done something good for Trigger. He lived to the ripe old age (for a horse) of 33.

TONS OF FUN

The biggest elephant ever? Probably Jumbo. He was the star of P.T. Barnum's circus in the 1880's. People came from far and wide to see Jumbo, whose height, at the shoulder, was 10 feet, 9 inches.

Barnum bought Jumbo in England. In the process, he almost caused a civil war. Jumbo lived in the London Zoo. Children loved to ride on Jumbo. Jumbo loved them right back. When he

was sold, the English, including Queen Victoria, were furious. But the deed was done, and Jumbo left for America. His trip wasn't easy. It took 15 days to cross the Atlantic by ship.

In America, Jumbo became Barnum's star attraction. More than one million children rode him in the next three years.

Then disaster struck. Jumbo was being led across railroad tracks. An unscheduled train roared along and hit and killed him.

At his death, Jumbo weighed more than 13,000 pounds. But when the veterinarian examined him, he found that Jumbo hadn't finished growing yet!

BIGGEST HAM ON BROADWAY

Can you picture a Broadway star gaining 600 pounds — and not losing his job? Here's one. It's Wilbur, the pig, who starred in the musical *King of Hearts* when it opened in New York in October, 1978.

Wilbur never expected special treatment. He wanted to be treated like any other star — and he was. He'd arrive at the theater in a limousine. He'd get his meals at a fine restaurant — without bacon, thank you. And he got high billing on the cast list.

When the show opened, the good wishes came rolling in. "Break a leg," said one telegram. Only one thing disturbed Wilbur. The show's co-producer, Joe Kipness, owns a famous New York restaurant. "If you're not a hit," Kipness warned Wilbur, "you could wind up on my menu."

When he's not working, Wilbur lives at Animal Actors, Inc., in Washington, New Jersey. There everyone's a star. Wilbur's next-door neighbor is a cougar who starred in another Broadway play, *The Magic Show.*

Soooo-ey, soooo-ey, superstar!

WORLD'S BUSIEST CAMEL

Talk about overtime. Here's the story of a 12-year-old who worked harder than anyone we know.

Her name: Lady Suzanne. And, on December

1, 1966, she was the busiest actress in New York City.

Lady Suzanne, you see, was a single-hump camel. And on that unforgettable (for her) day, she put in a rehearsal and four shows at Radio City Music Hall. And, as if that wasn't enough, she also appeared in an opera at Lincoln Center's Metropolitan Opera House.

How did she do it? First came the rehearsal and three performances of *The Nativity*, the Christmas stage show at Radio City. Then she jumped into a moving van, and, with a police escort, raced up to the Opera House where she took part in Samuel Barber's opera, *Antony and Cleopatra*.

Finally, after the opera, it was back into the van for the final show of *The Nativity*.

Camels are great on the desert. They can go for days without water. There's no word on the effects of long-term show business.

THE MIAMI DOLPHIN

There's nothing fishy about this story. It's about Flipper, star of movies, television, the Miami Seaquarium, and the Miami Dolphins football team.

But, as you fish experts know, the bottlenose dolphin (or porpoise) isn't a fish at all. He's a mammal. He's warm-blooded, has a brain and a high IQ, talks up a storm, and breathes air through a hole in the top of his head — just like his big uncle, the whale.

There have been several Flippers, most of them females. The first, Mitzi, starred in the two Flipper movies.

The second, Suzie, won everyone's heart in a long-running NBC television series.

Now, Flipper has two big jobs. One is performing daily at the Miami Seaquarium. The pay isn't much — three meals a day, including 15 pounds of fish plus vitamins. But there's one bonus. Every other Sunday during the fall, Flipper swims onto a special mattress and is covered with wet sheets. Then he gets into a truck bound for the Orange Bowl stadium. That's where he performs his second job — official dolphin for pro football's Miami Dolphins. Flipper works in a special exhibit tank and entertains the fans with his special brand of dolphin tricks.

Sure, it's work. But as hard as it is to get front-row seats for Miami football games, Flipper has the best seat in the house!

M-I-C, K-E-Y

An honorary place in *The Animal Hall of Fame* for a creature who's number one on everybody's animal list. Sure, the king of Disney World and Disneyland — Mickey Mouse.

When Mickey turned 50 in November, 1978, the whole country stopped to honor him. There was a TV special, a cross-country train trip, movies, record albums, magazine stories, and all kinds of Mickey souvenirs.

Walt Disney started the Mickey Mouse legend in 1928 when the little guy starred in *Steamboat Willie*. It was also the first sound cartoon. Mickey's voice was provided by Walt Disney himself.

It didn't take long for Walt and his people to develop other animal characters: Donald Duck, Pluto, Goofy, and all the rest. But No. 1? No doubt about it. It's Mickey Mouse!

WOULD YOU BELIEVE SENATOR GOOFY?

Some folks in Connecticut say the state is going to the dogs. Well, it isn't — exactly.

When state officials counted the votes for Connecticut's governor in 1978, among those receiving votes were Mickey Mouse, Minnie Mouse, Goofy, and the one and only Kermit the Frog.

Fortunately for Connecticut, Governor Ella Grasso got enough votes to win her second term in office.

BIG TALKER

One of TV's most popular series was really for the birds. The series: *Baretta*, starring Robert Blake. Make that co-starring Robert Blake. To many viewers, the real star was Fred, the super cockatoo.

Fred is like a great ballplayer. "He can do it all," say the scouts. "He talks on the phone, he barks like a dog, he waves, he screams. Everything."

The man who tells Fred what to do — most of the time — is Ray Berwick. He's Fred's trainer. Ray trains lots of birds.

"The producers of *Baretta* were looking for a mynah bird. I brought one. I also brought Fred. He was an instant hit. He got the job.

"Most cockatoos come from Australia or New Guinea," says Berwick. "Not Fred. I got him in a shipment of birds from Hong Kong. When I got

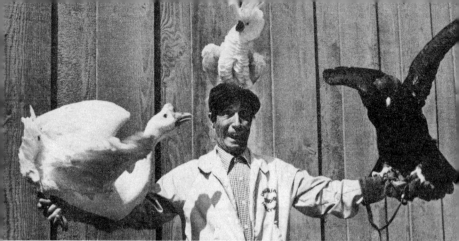

him, he spoke only one language — Chinese! I had to teach him English.

"The first English word he learned was 'Hello.' Then he learned 'I love you' and 'Give me a kiss.' So I gave him a kiss. Now, if you don't kiss him when he orders you to, he bites."

Biting is one of Fred's favorite pastimes. "He's a hard worker," reports Berwick. "The actors have to work hard, too. If they blow a cue, he'll bite them."

"Baretta" Blake was one of his victims. "Fred didn't like the way Robert was doing his part," remembers Berwick. Everyone, it seems, is a critic.

Actually, Fred and Blake were good friends. "They had to be," says Berwick. "The writers couldn't put Fred's part into the script. Robert and Fred (and I) worked out their tricks together. Fred is very smart. He was able to pick up a new trick in just a few minutes, sometimes on the first try."

One of Fred's greatest stunts is his imitation of a chicken. How did Berwick teach it to him?

"I didn't," says Berwick. "Fred must have done that on his own. All of a sudden, he just did it. I rewarded him with a treat. From then on, whenever I said 'chicken,' he went into the chicken routine."

What are Fred's favorite foods? Cookies, sunflower seeds, and — lasagna. "That's right," says Berwick. "The bird is an Italian food freak!"

Baretta was finally cancelled. That put Fred out of a $500 a week job. Chances are he'll be back. Cockatoos usually live to age 50 or 60. Fred, at age 12, is a baby. Fred shall talk again!

IDENTIFIED FLYING OBJECTS

It was easily one of the scariest movies ever. Those who saw it in the theater years ago remember it well. And those who see it on TV today are still terrified, thanks to the work of some of our animal friends.

The movie: Alfred Hitchcock's 1963 classic, *The Birds.*

It seemed that every bird — except the Balti-more Orioles — got work in the movie. In all, Hitchcock used more than 3,000 trained birds. There were all kinds: ravens, gulls, crows, ducks, finches, and more.

They had a bunch of birds flying down a chim-ney. But the finches they used didn't want to fly. They preferred to hang onto the side of the chim-ney. So the staff turned air hoses on the birds to *make* them fly.

Then they put some more finches into a glass cage. They flew around against a clear backdrop. They printed both pictures onto one frame of film. That gave them double the number of birds they really had.

The final scene was even harder to film — the filmmakers used 16 different shots of birds in one frame. It was very difficult.

Hollywood never runs out of camera tricks. In *The Birds*, there was an eye-in-the-sky shot over a gas station. It wasn't really real. Well, almost. One side of the shot was real. It was a seaside shot. The other side of the road was on the studio lot. They put the two shots together for the film.

There were lots of double shots in *The Birds*. One scene showed birds attacking children. It never really happened. The children were in one shot. The birds, who were photographed in the studio, were in another.

How do you get birds to rush to anywhere? Easy. Feed them. The staff of *The Birds* made great use of bird food.

Watch *The Birds* next time it's on your home

television. You'll be scared — but remember, though, that what you see isn't necessarily what you get!

. . . AND A TOOTHY GRIN

The biggest star at Universal Studios? The company has lots of big stars. But the biggest one is Bruce. No last name. Just Bruce. He weighs in at just about 3,000 pounds. Nobody does it "bigger."

You may have guessed that Bruce is no human. He's a shark — the star of *Jaws*. And he's not even a real shark. Universal couldn't take a chance on one of its stars eating up the rest of the cast. So it had to make a shark. If you've seen *Jaws* (or *Jaws II*), you know they did a great job.

In addition to his ton and a half weight (most of it machinery), Bruce was 15 feet long. Anyone

with that size would delight a basketball coach.

As an actor, Bruce had his problems. Like the time his powerful jaws got stuck. Or when he bashed the control panel with his head.

Eventually, Universal had to build three Bruces to do all the things the movie required him to do. It took 14 people — and 100 feet of cable — to keep him going.

The producers of *Jaws* used some real sharks in the movies, too. They used special film shot by a brave scientist in a special underwater shark cage.

All together, they made a very scary movie. But don't worry. It was only a movie. Chances are, it's perfectly safe to go in the water next summer — if you can swim!

AND THE ENVELOPE, PLEASE

Oscars, Emmys, Tonys? Bah, humbug. Anyone can win those awards. They're for people.

The Patsys are something else. They're the special awards for performing animals — and animal lovers. Since 1951, the American Humane Association has passed out gorgeous trophies to outstanding actors and actresses, mostly of the four-legged variety.

The winners provide a veritable catalog of the all-timers in the Hollywood animal kingdom. The first Patsy winner was Francis, the Talking Mule. Francis and his sidekick Donald O'Connor entertained millions. You could always separate Francis from his buddy. He was the smarter one.

Francis won the Patsy so often that he was

removed from competition and placed in the AHA's Animal Hall of Fame. The other Hall of Famers include: Lassie, Benji, Morris the Cat, and Scruffy, a famous dog.

Today's Patsy candidates compete in four categories: canine (dogs), equine (horses), wild animals, and "special." The first two categories speak for themselves. The other two require explanation.

Wild animals are those that are normally found in the wild. Recent nominees have included a sea lion, a tiger, and a chimpanzee. The 1978 winner was Farkas, the wolf in TV's *Lucan* series.

The special category includes anyone not in the first three groups, such as birds, goats, cats, etc. Example: Ben the Rat won the award twice.

The Hollywood branch of the American Humane Association oversees the Patsy Awards. They also keep a careful eye on the use of animals in TV and movies.

"More trained animals are being used in entertainment than ever before," says AHA Hollywood director Carmelita Pope. "We have three people working in the field full-time who watch everything in production. They make sure the animals are not being abused in any way."

How the Patsys got their name is the trivia question of the week. At first, it stood for Picture Animal Top Star of the Year. Later, when TV zoomed in popularity, a second set of Patsys began for the *Performing* Animal Television Star of the Year. Put either one together and it still comes out PATSY!

Unsung Heroes

What's next? It's the second "room" of our *Dynamite Animal Hall of Fame*. This time the honored guests are the unsung heroes. They're the animals that have done great things to help people — but haven't gotten nearly the credit they deserve. Well, they're getting the credit now!

THE BEAR TRUTH

He's about the most famous bear who ever lived. He spent more than 25 years helping to stamp out forest fires. And he gave his name, "Smokey," to a whole generation of C. B. radio users.

Smokey the Bear was found in the Lincoln National Forest during a forest fire in 1950. His parents had died in the fire and he was badly burned.

The forest ranger who found him brought the four-pound cub to his family. They nursed him back to health.

Within a few months, the cub grew too big for his adopted house. So the ranger's family gave him to the U. S. Forest Service. They named the bear "Smokey" after a cartoon bear already in use.

Smokey moved into the National Zoo in Washington. Eventually he grew to 300 pounds. Millions of people visited him and everyone remembered his message: "Only you can prevent forest fires!" It didn't take long for Smokey to become the No. 1 attraction in the zoo and one of the most popular — along with the Lincoln Memorial and the White House — in all of Washington.

Smokey died at age 25, but another orphan bear, Little Smokey, was ready to take his place.

The contribution to C. B. language? It was Smokey's hat. Since state troopers wear the same kind of forest ranger hat as Smokey, all highway police earned the slang title "Smokey."

IN HIGH PLACES

The President of the United States is the Chief Executive. His wife is the First Lady. What, then, should we call his pet. The country's Best Friend?

Almost every president has enjoyed the company of a pet. In fact, some preferred the company of their pets to their aides — or anyone else, for that matter.

President Zachary Taylor loved ponytails.

Only the tail he loved most was attached to his horse, Old Whitey. Taylor used to pluck tail hair for good luck.

President Warren Harding's dog, Laddie Boy, had his own seat at Cabinet meetings and enjoyed birthday parties with other dogs. The birthday cake? A pile of dog biscuits covered with special icing.

President Calvin Coolidge was known as "Silent Cal." But he wasn't silent when his pet cat, Tiger, disappeared. Coolidge got right on the radio — the first time any president used radio — and broadcast a missing cat report. Tiger turned up only a few blocks away.

President Theodore Roosevelt's daughter Alice kept one of the White House's most unusual pets, a snake named Emily Spinach.

Another Roosevelt, President Franklin D.,

spent more years (13) in the White House than any other president. That helped make Fala, his little pet Scottie, well-known to all Americans. During World War II, Fala became an honorary army private. How? By giving one dollar to the war effort. Thousands of other dogs across the country followed suit.

President Lyndon Johnson loved dogs. His favorite dogs were his beagles, Him and Her. Once he shocked the country by picking up the dogs by their ears.

President Richard Nixon and his family loved dogs. Nixon's was an Irish setter, King Timahoe. His daughters, Tricia and Julie, owned a terrier and poodle respectively.

But an earlier Nixon dog, Checkers, won worldwide fame. When he was running for vice-president in 1952, Nixon got into trouble on campaign funds. The then-senator from California went on radio and TV and pleaded innocent. At one point, though, he did admit accepting one gift from a political supporter. It was Checkers, his dog. The speech made Checkers a TV star and one of the most famous dogs in history!

But the all-time record for executive pets belongs to President John F. Kennedy and his family. During the Kennedy years, the White House played host to countless dogs, cats, parakeets, canaries, ducks, rabbits, guinea pigs, and ponies. It took a great sacrifice by the President to keep them all there. He was highly allergic to most animal fur.

SWING INTO SPRING

Need a weather forecast? You can listen to radio or TV or read your favorite newspaper. Or you can check the groundhog on Groundhog Day. He's rarely wrong.

The history of Groundhog Day is a little confusing. Actually, Groundhog Day isn't Groundhog Day. It's Candlemas Day. According to a Scottish

legend: "If Candlemas Day is bright and clear, there'll be two winters in the year."

The Romans picked up the tradition and passed it to the Germans who shipped it off to Pennsylvania. The earliest settlers in Pennsylvania, you see, were Germans. Now is that clear?

Anyhow, the folks in Punxsutawney, PA, claim to have the official, professional, big-league groundhog. Every February 2 since 1887, they've gone out to Gobbler's Knob and waited for their "Seer of Seers" to make his decision. As the legend goes, if the groundhog sees his shadow, winter will continue for six more weeks. If not, it will be an early spring.

That's only part of a gala groundhog festival in Punxsutawney. Day-long activities on February 2 wind up with a Groundhog Club dinner. You don't even have to go to Punxsutawney to join the Groundhog Club. There are chapters in Chicago, Detroit, Los Angeles, Pittsburgh, Washington, Houston, and a bunch of other places, too.

Do these folks take their groundhogs seriously? You'd better believe it. Here's their salute to their favorite little critter: "He stands supreme, imitated but unchallenged, envied but acknowledged, King of the Weather Prophets — Lord High Potentate of all Marmota Monas, and Wejack Extraordinary." If you're wondering what Marmota Monas and Wejack mean . . . actually they're both fancy names for groundhogs.

GOTCHA!

Most policemen think they're underpaid. But some officers work for dog biscuits — and love it.

Dog biscuits? Sure. These police officers are dogs, members of the K-9 corps employed by many police departments.

Years ago, the police used bloodhounds to track down criminals. Today, they use specially-trained German shepherds. The K-9 canines do a variety of jobs, including controlling crowds, preventing muggings, tracking criminals, and lots more.

The police dogs are unlike any pet you've ever seen. The dogs spend many months in training, learning to respond to commands and to react under pressure. The training is tough. Not all of the dogs who try it can make it. It takes a special kind of dog to become a police dog.

New York City's police department uses its dogs strictly for bomb detection. "A big city like ours has lots of security problems," said the man in charge of the NYPD's bomb squad. "You can't imagine what we have to go through when, for example, the president comes to town. That's when our dogs really come in handy."

How sharp is the dog's sense of smell? "It's unbelievable," said our man at the NYPD. "Their smelling ability is about 750 times sharper than a human's. And the object in question doesn't even have to be around. The dogs can work on a leftover odor."

The New York police dogs have performed

some really heroic feats. "They saved hundreds of lives one day in 1971," remembered our expert. "A bomb was reported aboard a TWA jetliner. We sent our men in; they couldn't find anything. Then we brought in the dogs. They put their hands— make that their noses— on it right away. If that plane had taken off,

there's no telling how many lives might have been lost!"

Though New York City uses its dogs only on bomb searches, the K-9's are used in other jobs elsewhere. New York State's police force employs bloodhounds to trail criminals. Philadelphia uses them in crowd control. Various Southern states have the dogs perform patrol duties.

The Federal Aviation Agency uses dogs in firearms control. And United States Customs makes use of its dogs to detect illegal drugs. The advantage? The officers don't have to open every package. The dogs tell them which ones contain the drugs.

How are New York City's dogs trained?

"That's a professional secret," said the head man at the NYPD bomb squad. "But, remember this, in all the years we've been using dogs here, they've never made a mistake."

By the way, police dogs, like police officers, don't really work for dog biscuits. They get a super-high-protein diet, with plenty of eggs, cheese, and meat. In fact, that's a lot better than some human policemen eat.

WHAT'S UP, DOX?

It's hard being a police officer. The work is difficult and, at times, dangerous. But there are rewards, too. Many police officers retire and enjoy their old age.

What would you think, then, of a police officer

who was still working at age 98? Incredible — and true.

This police officer also happened to have four legs and a tail. His name was Dox and, of course, he was a dog. Not just any dog, mind you, but the Italian police force's number-one German shepherd. Year after year, Dox was Europe's champion police dog. He won four gold medals and 21 silver medals during a long, extraordinary career. He was still working at age 14 — the same as a 98-year-old man.

Dox could do just about anything a two-legged police officer could do — and then some.

A victim was tied up with rope? No problem. Dox could untie any and all knots.

A loaded pistol? Easy as pie. Dox could unload it after putting on the safety with his paws and teeth.

Dox did amazing things with his nose. Once, in a restaurant, he jumped on a man who was eating his dinner. Dox's master, Sgt. Giovanni Maimone, started shouting at Dox. The man, covered with spaghetti, was very upset.

But for Dox, it was just another job. He had sniffed the man's scent six years earlier and he remembered it. (Dox always remembered faces and scents.) As usual, he was right. The man in the restaurant was wanted by the police — and they hadn't found him in six years.

No burglar was ever safe with Dox around. He could pin the blame on any thief with a tiny clue that only he could find. Once he nabbed a jewel robber by finding a raincoat button in the jewelry store, and then matching it to the raincoat in the thief's closet. What a dog!

Another time, Dox saved Sgt. Maimone's life by pouncing on a thief who had snuck up on the sergeant with a knife.

During his career, Dox solved more than 400 cases for Rome's police department. His death was a crushing blow to the entire city. After all, how many humans did they have to hire to take his place?

A HELPING EYE

We all know that dogs are called "man's best friend," but to blind people a dog is more than a friend. Their dogs are their eyes.

One of the biggest training organizations for these life-saving canines is The Seeing Eye, which began providing dogs for the blind in 1929.

The organization's dogs are trained in Morristown, New Jersey. But they're available, at nominal cost, to blind Americans everywhere.

Most of the dogs are German shepherds. But golden and Labrador retrievers are also used. Other dogs also make good substitute eyes. Both male and female dogs are used.

The dogs' average life span is about 10 years, though some have lived and worked to age 13 or more. They eat almost any good dog food.

The dogs are usually around 14 months old when their training begins. First they work for about three months with their teachers. They learn basic obedience. They are taught to ignore distractions, such as children at play, other dogs, cats, etc.

Next they learn how to "say" no! If their master asks them to do something that might be dangerous, they must disobey. But they learn to do it intelligently.

Then the dogs go into the field. They are tested, under strict conditions, to be sure that they know how to be responsible for a human life. The dogs work at busy street corners and in heavy traffic. Sometimes the instructor is blindfolded. That makes the test even more realistic.

When the dog finally passes all of the tests, he's ready for his final lessons — with his new master. That phase of learning takes another

four weeks. The blind person learns about his dog; the dog learns about his master. They work in small classes as the master learns each of the dog's movements.

After that, all it takes is practice. The dog and master walk around all sorts of obstacles — low-hanging tree branches, broken sidewalks, and so on. They learn how to get onto a bus, how to walk in a store or restaurant, etc.

What drives the dogs and their owners crazy? It's not traffic, or curbs, or almost any usual day-to-day problem. It's people. If someone takes hold of the dog or distracts him, it disrupts the teamwork between dog and master.

THEY'RE ALL EARS!

Almost everyone has heard of seeing-eye dogs. But did you know that some deaf people can "hear" again, thanks to specially-trained dogs?

They're called "hearing dogs" and they're trained by the American Humane Association. The dogs are taught to listen to the sounds that deaf persons should be aware of.

Is the phone ringing? Is the doorbell chiming? Is the alarm clock buzzing? Is a fire alarm clanging? Is the baby crying?

Those are the kinds of sounds a hearing dog listens for. When he hears them, he makes contact with his deaf master.

The first hearing-dog training program is being conducted in Denver, Colorado. Any kind of dog can be used as a hearing dog.

How can you tell a hearing dog from a standard pet? The hearing dog is the one wearing the bright orange collar or leash!

JUST WILD ABOUT BARRY

It snows a lot in the Swiss Alps. And tons of snow spells tons of trouble for travelers. Nowadays, most of them go by car and can be picked up in helicopters. But 150 years ago, most of them moved about on foot. And got lost on foot.

Enter the St. Bernard. He's a huge dog and can get places that others — dogs *and* people — can't. During the early 1800's, a whole team of St. Bernard rescue dogs worked in the Alps. And none was more famous than Barry.

Every day, for 12 years, he was on the job. He was always on the lookout for people trapped in the snow. According to reports, Barry saved at least 40 people. He could almost sense when someone was in trouble.

The famous picture of a St. Bernard with a barrel of brandy around his neck isn't true. But the legend of the St. Bernard's great life-saving acts is.

Everyone was just wild about Barry — and all his friends, too.

TO SAVE A LIFE

If you visit Alaska today, you'll be amazed. The far-off north land is a bustling state. It's just like any of the other 49 states, just a little colder.

It wasn't always that way. In January, 1925,

Alaska was practically all frozen wasteland. In the winter, the city of Nome was cut off from the rest of the world, being hundreds of miles from the nearest railroad terminal.

That's what created the biggest problem when the dread disease, diphtheria, broke out. People, mostly children, were getting sick and even dying. The life-saving medicine was hard to find. And even if it could be found, someone would have to get it to Nome. That was the real problem.

Then came the first miracle. Anti-toxin serum, which would save some lives and prevent others from getting sicker, was found in Anchorage. It could be taken by train to Nenanna, Alaska. But that was nearly 700 miles from Nome. The only way to get it to Nome was by dogsled.

The chances of the trip being completed safely were slim. It would take skilled sled drivers, brave sled dogs, smart lead dogs, and, most important, tremendous good luck for the effort to succeed. But since there was really no other way, the job was begun.

One group of drivers started from the train. Another set started from Nome. Their job would be hardest. The second part of the journey would be made in incredibly bad weather.

The dogs were strong and tough. Some of them were huskies. Others were Alaskan malamutes. Still others were half-dog, half-wolf. All of them had wide chests, short necks, and, of course, powerful legs.

The serum had gone 500 miles from the train at

Nenanna when the first team of dogs from Nome met it. This team was driven by Leonhard Seppala. He was 170 miles from home, 170 miles from stopping the diphtheria epidemic.

The temperature was 30 degrees below zero. The wind was howling at more than 50 miles per hour. The cold was inhuman. The snow made it impossible for man or beast to see more than a few feet. The driver and his brave dogs cut across a frozen bay before completing their leg of the journey, a total of 90 miles. Now the serum was only 80 miles from Nome.

The weather got worse. Charlie Olson drove the next team. It took many hours, but he got through. Half-frozen, he passed the package of life-saving serum to Gunnar Kaasen.

Kaasen had the hardest job of all. He also had one of the best lead dogs, a Siberian husky named Balto. Together they went off into the night, 13 dogs and one man.

With Balto in the lead, Kaasen managed to avoid problems. One time he even fell off the sled, losing the precious serum in the process. Fortunately he found it moments later. When Kaasen's relief driver failed to show up, he and his team mushed right on through to Nome. Six-and-a-half hours later they made it. It ended one of the most courageous animal stories ever.

The entire 670-mile trip from Nenanna had taken just under six days. It was a miracle. Thanks to the serum (and more that arrived by ship later) the diphtheria outbreak was stopped with no more deaths.

HOME, SWEET HOME

Did you ever get lost? Really lost? Then you found out that you were only a short distance from home? Sure. It has happened to everyone.

But not to the carrier or homing pigeon. You can take one of those birds up to 1,000 miles (or, in some cases, more) from home and they'll fly right back. These on-target flyers can best be used to deliver messages. Better than the mail or telegraph, the only way to stop a carrier-pigeon message is to shoot the bird down.

Paul Julius Reuter (say it ROY-ter) knew all about homing pigeons. And he made it pay off.

In 1849, the telegraph system in Europe stretched from Paris, France, to Brussels, Belgium. Another arm stretched from Berlin, Germany, to Aachen in Prussia.

That created problems for stockbrokers in Berlin who wanted the Paris prices. It took nine hours for the train to go from Brussels to Aachen.

How to solve the problem? Paul Julius Reuter had the answer. Homing pigeons. The "40 well-trained birds" were taken to Brussels where they would receive their messages (attached to their legs). The messages contained the Paris stock prices. Then the birds would fly home to Aachen. They could make the trip seven hours faster than the train.

So important was Reuter's information that he locked all his customers into a room so that none of them would get (and use) the information before any of the others.

Today, the Reuters News Service uses satellites and computers to spread its words. But it all started with Paul Julius and his birds.

LOOKING LIKE A MILLION

What do millionaires eat? Steak, lobster, caviar? Sure. But some millionaires prefer hay and oats and good stuff like that. Most of those millionaires, of course, have four legs.

You guessed it. They're horses. And some of them have made more money than any two-legged folks you know.

Take Kelso. He raced until he was nine years old. And he didn't waste time, either. He earned $1,977,896 for his owners. Right behind came Forego. He made $1,938,869.

Some of the other rich horses include: Round Table ($1,749,869), Dahlia ($1,543,139), and Exceller ($1.5 million and counting).

Those are the horses that brought home the bacon. But some other horses made their owners even richer. They were sold to horse breeders. The champion so far: Seattle Slew, $12 million.

Money, of course, is only part of the horse story. Races today pay more money than ever before. Some of the all-time greats raced when the purses (prize money) were low.

Here are some of the greatest horses of all time:

Exterminator. The first race he ever ran was the 1918 Kentucky Derby. Guess what? He won it! Was it a fluke? Nope. In all, Exterminator ran 100 times, winning 50 of them. He ran in three countries, at distances from 5½ furlongs (about three-quarters of a mile) to three miles. Nothing ever bothered him.

Gallant Fox. He raced only 17 times, finishing in the top three all but once (when he was distracted watching an airplane when the race started). Three of his wins came in the Triple Crown — Kentucky Derby, Preakness, and Belmont Stakes. Then his son, Omaha, won the Triple Crown, too. No other Triple winner has ever fathered another Triple winner!

Secretariat. No one had won the Triple Crown for 25 years when Secretariat did it in 1973. In the

Kentucky Derby, he was left at the gate and started last. Slowly he started to catch up. He went from 11th to sixth after a half mile, to fifth after three-quarters. In the last eighth of a mile, he passed his last horse, won the race, and set a new record. Secretariat was a lazy horse; he never ran for the first half mile. But when he got going, nothing could stop him.

Man O' War was probably the greatest horse ever. He ran 21 times and lost only once (he came in second). He won almost every race easily, setting record after record. In one outing, the 1920 Lawrence Realization at Belmont, "Big Red" set a new world record for 1⅝ miles. By the way, he won the race by an unbelievable 100 lengths!

EARNING HIS STRIPES

Millions of Americans go to the races every year. They love seeing the horses tearing around the track. But what about the zebras?

Yes, Virginia, there is a racing zebra. Thanks to the patience of veteran trainer Jim Papon, a zebra was trained to race at Florida's Pompano Park.

What made the job hard was the special gait required of trotters, even trotting zebras. It took months to teach the zebra to run properly, then more time to show him how to use the sulky. That's the little cart that trotting horses — and zebras — pull behind them.

But Jim Papon's hard work paid off. The zebra, named the Stanleyville Steamer, actually raced at Pompano. And, though he finished second (to a real trotter) in a two-animal race, he instantly became the world's first — and fastest — trotting zebra!

IT'S A LIVING!

A few animals have it good. They work on TV or they race around a track a few times. But many working animals work harder — and for much less. They're the animals who help in science labs. The real unsung heroes of the animal world.

About 45 million rats and mice usually give their lives for you — and science — every year. So do around 20 million frogs.

Birds come next with almost two million, followed by hamsters, rabbits, and guinea pigs, with nearly a half-million apiece. Without their help, scientists would not be able to do the research that may cure diseases and save lives. So it seems appropriate for *The Dynamite Animal Hall of Fame* to say: "Thanks, guys!"

Animal People

Some pets are people's best friends. And, believe it or not, some people are animals' best friends. In this part of our *Hall of Fame*, we salute those two-legged "animals" who have done great things for those with four (or more) legs.

MR. UNDERWATER

Few fish live to a ripe old age. Jacques-Yves Cousteau, however, is still going strong at close to 70.

Jacques isn't a fish, you say. You're right, of course. But he spends more time underwater than most of them. Officially, Jacques is an oceanographer. But he's more than that. He's an undersea explorer, a pioneer, an inventor, and a TV star. And more.

Born in France in 1910, Jacques wasn't very healthy. His doctors told him not to work too hard. He didn't listen — fortunately for the rest of us. He learned to swim and also learned to love the sea. He also showed he had a great mind for science.

He first began underwater swimming and experiments in 1936. He had seen a Chinese fisherman dive under the water without equipment and catch fish in his bare hands. That got Jacques going.

Not long afterward, he invented (with another man) the Aqua-Lung. He made several underwater films. And, finally, in 1952, he made his first trip in his research ship, the *Calypso*. The result of that maiden voyage — under the Red Sea — were the first color pictures ever shot at 150 feet deep.

Things happened quickly after that. Cousteau wrote many books, all telling stories of his underwater adventures. He won three Oscars for his fabulous movies. And then, in 1966, he made his first television special. He hasn't been off the tube since.

With *Calypso* as his base, Jacques has taken photos under deep, unknown parts of the sea. He has also done weather experiments, some of which helped the U. S. space program. And he and his men have lived and worked for a month, 40 feet under the sea, on the continental shelf.

Cousteau is a businessman, too. He is the head of an organization called the Cousteau Group. It is really 16 companies in all sorts of businesses, all around the world. One of them — no surprise — makes movies and TV films.

Anyone who is interested in undersea activities can learn something from Cousteau's TV shows. He has devoted whole hours to the sharks, the green sea turtle, the walrus, the whale, and the penguin, among others. TV star Cousteau has won both Peabody and Emmy awards for his programs.

"I love television," says Jacques. "Lots of people see my movies and read my books. But there's nothing like TV. On any night, you know that 35 or 40 million people are watching and learning."

At six feet tall and 154 pounds, Jacques is always in shape. "Physical fitness is all important," he says. And, while he has two homes in Europe, the place he prefers to live is on the sea — on the *Calypso*.

KING OF THE WILD KINGDOM

For most folks, having their own TV show is a full-time job. Not for Marlin Perkins. He has taught three generations of TV watchers all about animals.

But that wasn't all he did. For years, while he was starring on *Zoo Parade* and, later, *Wild Kingdom* on NBC-TV, Perkins was a working zoo director.

Born in 1905, Marlin got his first job (after graduating from the University of Missouri) at the St. Louis Zoo. He swept the walks, trimmed the

hedges, and cleaned the grounds. He was paid $18 a week.

In 1962, with 36 years of experience behind him, he was named *director* of the same zoo. His pay was just a little higher.

Perkins — and his animal friends — were among the earliest TV stars. "It all started in 1945," he remembers. "I was the director of the Lincoln Park Zoo in Chicago. The director of the TV station asked me to bring some animals down to the station. It wasn't much. At the time, there were only 300 TV sets in the area.

"It was easy. And it must have worked well. They called us more and more often. We'd bring the animals down and we'd stay on the air until we — or the animals — had enough."

Actually, Perkins was very good. By 1950, he was the star of Zoo Parade. It was a coast-to-coast favorite on NBC. Since 1963, he and his staff have been doing Wild Kingdom.

One reason why Perkins has succeeded is his sense of humor. Once, to win over some antelopes, he dressed up like an ostrich. He ran up and down with the antelopes, skipping as an ostrich would.

Perkins is pretty brave, too. Once he dived into a school of Australian sharks. All he had to protect himself was a stick. He used it to smack their snouts. Yes, "snouts."

"It was good to find out," he said, "that these sharks wouldn't eat just *anything*."

Teacher, naturalist, zoo director, TV star. Marlin Perkins has done it all!

MONKEY LADY

From the time she was born, in England in 1934, Jane Goodall was interested in animals. There was little doubt that she'd spend her life working with them.

When she was 23 she made her first trip to Africa. To Tanzania. That's where she decided to work. She felt that studying chimpanzees might give clues as to how ancient people behaved.

That's exactly what she did. She got some help from two sources: first, the Wilkie Foundation agreed to pay her expenses; second, her mother

agreed to work with her in Africa. It was a perfect team.

The work wasn't easy. Jane had to survive the jungle with its wild beasts, as well as the problems of disease. But after months of waiting, she finally got together with the chimps. They hit it off immediately.

Jane gave them names, like "Baby Flint," "Mr. McGregor," and "David Greybeard." She tried to learn all of their habits. To do this, she did things just as they did. She spent a lot of time in trees. She ate the kinds of food they ate, including some insects.

She learned a lot. But two of her discoveries were most important.

First, some people felt that chimps were vegetarians. That was wrong. Jane found that they kill and eat insects, chickens, and even baboons and some monkeys.

Second, she found that humans weren't the only mammals that made tools. The chimps did, too. They used them to dig, eat, and more.

She also learned that chimps can throw stones with some accuracy, that they can walk more upright than was formerly believed, and that they enjoyed an active social life.

Much of Jane's work was lonely. It had to be. But she was rarely alone. One of her visitors was Baron Hugo van Lawick, a Dutch wild-animal photographer. He did his job — then stayed around. When he and Jane were married in 1964, she became the Baroness van Lawick-Goodall.

"I'm sure the chimps don't think much of me," she said once. "They rank me with the baboons. But they know that I can produce all the bananas they need."

A MAN AND HIS BEAR

Dan Haggerty. "Grizzly" Adams. They are the same. Haggerty starred as Adams in an *NBC Monday Night Movie* and, later, in an NBC series. And it was special, because Haggerty and his animal friends enjoyed a special relationship.

Why did NBC pick Dan Haggerty for the part of "Grizzly" Adams? Partly because of his acting ability. Partly because of his love for animals.

Actually, Dan started out as an animal trainer. He sold his furniture to buy his first lion cub. He spent a year in Brazil supervising animals for *Tarzan* TV shows.

At 6-1 and 195 pounds, Haggerty is a bear of a man. "I guess I owe it all to my animals," he says. "They put me where I am today. Nature has been good to me."

KENYA DIG IT?

How's your pet lion? You mean you don't have one? George and Joy Adamson had one. Their pet lioness was named Elsa. And, as the "star" of the popular movie *Born Free*, Elsa was one of the best-loved animals of all time.

The Adamsons, of course, lived in Kenya (in Africa). George Adamson was a game warden. One day he was attacked by a wild lioness and had to kill her. Unfortunately, she left three days-old cubs.

So George and Joy Adamson began raising the tiny lions. At first, they looked more like kittens than lions. The little lions drank milk from cans and played with toys.

It didn't take long for the lions to grow much bigger. After only five months, the Adamsons had to send the two largest ones to the zoo.

"We don't really like to do that," said Mr. Adamson. "It's not really fair to have wild animals raised in a zoo." But there was no real choice.

The third lion was different. The Adamsons named her Elsa. They decided to get her ready to go back into the jungle where she belonged.

It wasn't easy. Elsa had never seen a lion kill to get its food or kill to protect itself. She had always lived with humans. It was up to the Adamsons to get her to act like — well, a lion!

It took nearly two years. Elsa was a natural stalker. She knew how to trail after what she wanted. But the Adamsons had to teach her to kill. Joy and George didn't want to rush Elsa. If she couldn't fend for herself, it could be very dangerous. Besides, they really loved her.

Finally, Elsa was ready. She was 27 months old. The Adamsons took her far from her home. They released her. But it didn't work well. Elsa wasn't used to the weather or the ground conditions.

When they brought her back closer to home, Elsa did much better. She was able to take care of herself in the jungle. She found a mate and even had three "children" — Jespah, Gopa, and Little Elsa. Elsa and her offspring came to visit the Adamsons often.

"Too many animals have been taken from the jungle," said Joy Adamson. "We'd like to make sure that there will always be plenty of animals in Africa."

That's why all the money the Adamsons made from their books and movies went into the Elsa Wild Animal Fund. What a nice thing to do for someone you love!

A DOG'S LIFE

Do you belong to a club? The Boys' Club? The Girl Scouts? Or maybe an Officially Official Dynamite Club?

Dogs belong to a club too — the American Kennel Club. The people who run the AKC deserve an honorary spot in *The Animal Hall of*

Fame. They are serious animal people who ever since 1884 have kept tabs on dog breeding.

The membership records of the AKC tell a revealing story. The most popular breed right now is the poodle. More than 100,000 of them were signed up at AKC headquarters the last time we looked. Next come Doberman pinschers, German shepherds, cocker spaniels, and Irish setters.

More than 120 different kinds of dogs are registered with the AKC. In all, more than a million dogs are on the books.

You can probably guess some of the more popular breeds. They include Labrador retrievers, beagles, dachshunds, golden retrievers, Shetland sheepdogs, miniature schnauzers, collies, lhasa apsos, and Yorkshire terriers.

Among the rarer breeds registered by AKC are English foxhounds, Sussex spaniels, har-

riers, field spaniels, Belgian malinois, curly-coated retrievers, otter hounds, clumber spaniels, and the ever-popular affenpinschers. There weren't as many as 100 of the above breeds on the most recent AKC membership list.

For purposes of show, dogs are divided into different groups. Working dogs are the most popular (more than 300,000 of the million AKC members). Then come sporting dogs, non-sporting dogs, hounds, toys, and terriers.

One word of caution to dog-show beginners: working dogs don't earn a living, sporting dogs don't play football, and toy dogs don't have batteries (not included)!

THE CROAKING CHORUS

So your dog doesn't look like Benji or Lassie. So you're not about to live under water for a month! Don't worry. You might still get your chance to be a famous animal person.

You might have the champion frog at the world-famous Calaveras County Frog Jumping Contest. No joke. People come from thousands of miles away to take a chance.

Mark Twain first told the story of "The Celebrated Jumping Frog" in an 1865 story. Since 1928, Twain's famous contest has been repeated every year in Angels Camp, California.

The contest is part of the annual Calaveras County Fair. Can you win a big prize? You certainly can. If your frog beats the world record, you get $1,200. Tie the world record and it's $500.

Other prizes range from $300 (for first place) down to $5 for eighth.

It costs two dollars for an adult to enter the annual contest. (Junior division entry costs 25 cents.) Your frog must be four inches long. He may take three jumps. His distance is measured from the starting point of jump one to the finishing point of jump three.

You don't have a pet frog? No matter. The folks at the contest will lend you one. They'll even lend you a jockey.

To get a frog going, a jockey will kick, stomp, yell, or do almost anything.

The current record-holder is "E. Davey Croakett" of Santa Clara, California. He and his jockey, Denny Matasci, managed a triple leap of 20 feet, three inches in 1976.

Do you think you can win? Why not? You can get an entry blank (or a Rent-a-Frog application) from the Jumping Frog Jubilee, PO Box 96, Angels Camp, CA 95222.

THE VOICE OF THE TURTLES

Frogs don't do it for you, you say? Well, if you have a dollar you can join the Turtles International Association, Ltd. The five and a half million members are people who agree that "Turtles are bright-eyed, bushy-tailed, fearless and unafraid folk with a fighter pilot attitude. They think clean, have fun a lot, and recognize the fact that you never get anyplace worthwhile in life unless you stick your neck out." Turtles

International sponsors special events such as the International Turtle Creepstakes. They sell souvenirs, even a Turtle newspaper. Any profits the group makes go to help handicapped children.

Unlike regular turtles, however, none of the members of Turtles International are known to have a shell.

WHO'S ZOO?

Looking for a zoo? You usually won't have far to look. There are more than 150 zoos of various shapes and sizes all across the country. Some are privately owned or contain just a couple of hundred animals or just animals of a certain variety.

Other zoos are enormous affairs, with

thousands of specimens across acres and acres of land.

Which are the best? That's not a fair question. It depends upon what you're looking for. If you have a special interest, one zoo might be just right for you — but not for someone else!

For general interest, however, there are a few outstanding zoos. Alphabetically, they include: Chicago's Lincoln Park Zoo, the Cincinnati Zoo, the Cleveland Zoo, Los Angeles's Griffith Park Zoo, New York's Bronx Zoo, the Philadelphia Zoo, the St. Louis Zoo, and the Washington (D.C.) National Zoo, home of the pandas sent to the U.S. as a gift of the People's Republic of China.

Did we leave out an important choice? We sure

did. It's the famed San Diego Zoo, our choice for No. 1 in the country.

The San Diego Zoo, which is more than 60 years old, owns the largest group of mammals, birds, and reptiles in the world. Everything in the zoo is done in a natural setting. There are no standard cages and pits, the kinds of things you see at lesser zoos.

The visitors — more than three million every year — can see over 1,000 different types of birds from every continent. And since it rarely rains in San Diego, the visitors can usually watch in comfort.

There are over 100 acres of zoo in San Diego. For the first-time visitor, we suggest the bus tour. You'll see every corner of the place.

Watch the bears. When the bus drives past, they may just sit up and wave.

Don't feed any of the animals. They're all on special diets. The reptiles eat crickets. The birds eat worms. The zoo supplies just the right amount of food for every resident. The zoo's yearly grocery list includes 10,000 crickets and 780,000 worms!

There's an animal nursery where the baby animals get special attention. Many animals raised at the San Diego Zoo have never been raised in captivity anywhere else.

The ape house, with orangutans, chimps, and monkeys, is a popular San Diego attraction. And no visit would be complete without a visit to the unique Children's Zoo.

The San Diego Zoo is the greatest!

OLD ZOOS ARE GOOD NEWS

The world's oldest zoo? Probably Vienna, Austria's Schonbrunn Zoo.

It has been doing business (as a zoo) at the same old spot for more than 200 years. Before that, the site played host to a deer park for another 200 years!

Strange Tales (and Strange Tails)

Did you ever want to know about some of the weird things animals do? You've come to the right place. The final "room" here at *The Dynamite Animal Hall of Fame* is devoted to the strange goings-on in the animal world. Come on in!

BEETLE 007

Secret agent James Bond has nothing on the bombardier beetle. When he's frightened by a close attack he discharges a liquid that instantly turns to gas in the air.

That puff of smoke (accompanied by a "Pop!" sound) distracts the enemy so the beetle can disappear.

HAZARDOUS TO HIS HEALTH

Snakes, it turns out, can be their own worst enemy. When enraged, they'll bite anything — including themselves. Their own venom can't kill them; they're immune to it. But if it penetrates their hearts, it's all over.

Do snakes really commit suicide? Their psychiatrists haven't told us yet.

EATING OUT

The plover is a long-legged bird with a very simple diet. It eats the uneaten food, insects, and leeches that it finds on the teeth of crocodiles.

The croc is asleep when the plover dines. His mouth is open as he naps in the sun, and the plover just makes himself right at home.

How can the plover take chances on picking the croc's teeth clean? The bird just isn't one of the croc's favorite foods.

HAVE TUX, WILL BABY-SIT

Day-care centers are springing up all across

America. They enable a lot of mothers to get back to work.

But penguins have been using the idea for years. The youngest birds are grouped together and cared for by the older penguins. Meanwhile the youngsters' parents are at work, hunting for food for all.

Incidentally, penguins aren't the only birds in the day-care business. Eider ducks have been doing it for years, too.

DESSERT IS WHERE IT'S AT&T

What's your favorite snack? Pizza? Hot dogs? Tacos?

For the gopher who lives in western America, the preferred food is vegetable roots. But when he's really hungry, he digs down even deeper and sinks his sharp teeth into lead-coated telephone wires.

We tried to ask the gopher why he enjoyed the wires. But, of course, his line was busy!

I'D WALK A MILE

The secret of survival is water. People can make it without food for some time. But water is a must.

Not for the camel. He's called "The Ship of the Desert," and for good reason. He can go for up to a week in the steamy desert without a drop.

His secret? His stomachs — that's right, stomachs — are lined with millions of tiny water storage cells. He can store enough to last for days.

He has one more great talent. In the desert, he can sniff out water holes. That's one talent that can save lives!

BEWARE THE SPITTER

Here's a piece of sound advice: Don't get a llama angry. The beast of burden from South America strikes back, literally, through its teeth. He'll spit a shower of saliva at anyone who bothers him.

It isn't any better if you're on his back, riding him. He'll just turn his head around and get you.

OPOSSUM A CHICKEN

For many animals, danger raises them to new heights of courage. Not the opossum.

When he confronts danger, he doesn't run. He just drops to the ground, nearly closes his eyes, lets his mouth drop open, and allows his tongue to hang out. He almost completely stops breathing. He looks and acts dead. His enemy often goes away.

It must work. The art of "playing possum" has made the opossum world-famous.

EGGS-ACTLY RIGHT

How do you like your eggs? You like two for breakfast, scrambled? You're on.

Now here's a way to cut down on the number of eggs you use. Try ostrich eggs. The North African ostrich produces enormous eggs. The largest average about six inches in circumference and weigh nearly four pounds. The shell is more than half an inch thick and is strong enough to support the weight of O.J. Simpson.

Now for the other side of the coin, er, frying pan. The smallest egg comes from the hummingbird. It's less than half an inch around and weighs around one-fifth of an ounce. O.J. Simpson could eat about a million of 'em.

WHAT AN OMELETTE!

In 1956, a New Jersey white leghorn laid the largest chicken egg ever. It weighed one pound!

ALL IN THE FAMILY

What's a big family? Six children? Seven? Eight?

That's nothing for a termite family. All of the children in a wood-eating colony come from one parent — the queen.

A healthy queen can live for as long as 50 years. Few insects live nearly as long.

Her daily output of eggs can reach as high as 25 or 30 thousand. That means that throughout her life, she can be mother to almost half a billion little termites.

THE THREE G'S

The worst spelling for any animal's name is the gnu. Of course, that's pronounced NOO. Another mispronounced non-human is the tiny gnat. Gno, you're wrong. That's pronounced NAT.

Those two are well off when you consider the plight of the giraffe. You know how to pronounce that, of course. But giraffes have a worse problem. They can't talk. That, however, keeps their telephone bill pretty low!

HIGH-FLYING SOCIETY

What do the rich people do? They stay warm. They follow the sun. Do they freeze during winter? No, sir. They head for the sandy beaches wherever the sun is hot.

So do the swallows. At least the square-tailed cliff swallows do. And how they do it makes a super story.

The swallows spend every winter in Argentina. Then, on exactly March 19, the swallows come home. Home is the town of San Juan Capistrano. That's in sunny southern California.

The birds spend a wonderful warm California summer. Then, on October 23, they pack up and go back to Argentina (where our winter is their summer). Not a bad life.

The swallows don't exactly show up unannounced on March 19. First come a flight of scout birds. They check the old sites, repair old nests, and build new ones. It's like having a summer home at the beach.

The swallows love to eat insects. Mother birds feed them to their young. They pluck the insects right out of the air with great speed and grace. What makes these tiny birds move from continent to continent every year at the same time? The scientists have some good guesses. But none of them are sure. If they ever find out, it's going to spoil a terrific story.

GROUP RATES

When more than two or three people get together, we say, "There's a crowd of people," or "a bunch of people," or "a lot of people." Get the idea?

We can do that for animals too. But there's a better way. Animal groups have special names. And most of them sound terrific.

A group of lions, for example, is actually a *pride of lions.*

A bunch of geese is really a *gaggle of geese.*

And when you see a slew of goldfinches flying around, it's better to say a *charm of goldfinches.*

Want to hear some more?

There's a *tribe* of *goats*, a *span* of *mules*, a *sleuth* of *bears*, and a *litter* of *pigs*.

Gorillas come in *bands*, cattle come in *droves*, elks come in *gangs*, and whales arrive in *pods*.

A group of fish, of course, is a *school*. A bunch of gnats? A *horde*. A lot of cats? A *clutter*. A team of leopards? A *leap*.

The prettiest names? We like these:

A *mute* of *hounds*.

A *volery* of *birds*.

A *muster* of *peacocks*.

A *congregation* of *plovers*.

A *kendle* of *kittens*.

A *covey* of *quail*.

And an *exaltation* of *larks*.

SNOW JOB

Mary Snow loved animals. She loved them when she was alive. And she loved them after she died. In her will, she gave her pet horses $32,000 so that they could be cared for. She left her pet dogs $1,000 each.

She left Mr. Snow — nothing!

The Animal Name Game

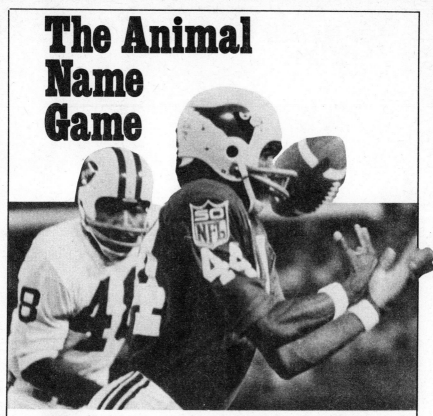

Before we close the doors on *The Animal Hall of Fame*, we should pause a moment and consider one other important contribution that animals have made to our life. Animals have graciously loaned their names time and time again to everything from football coaches (Bear Bryant) to dances (remember the Pony?).

SONG BIRDS — AND OTHER ANIMALS

Want to see The Eagles, The Good Rats, or The Fabulous Poodles? You don't have to go to a zoo. Visit your favorite record store.

They are all singing groups. And they're not the only animals in the history of show biz.

You might prefer The Hounds. Or The Animals. How about Buffalo Springfield or Country Joe and the Fish?

There are The Byrds. And other birds — The Robins, The Orioles, The Pelicans, The Flamingos, The Ravens, Hummingbird, and Mallard. Maybe Crow, The Blue Jays, or The Hawks are more your style.

Birds aren't your thing? On dry land you'll find The Groundhogs, The Turtles, and The Chipmunks. Scarier groups include Dragon, Rhinoceros, and Scorpion.

Even old fossils such as the sound of Tyrannosaurus Rex (or, as their friends called 'em, T-Rex).

Looking for a far-out group? There's The Spiders from Mars, which is about as far-out as you're going to get.

That's not all, of course. You remember Frampton's Camel, The Sharks, Foxy, Catfish, and zillions more. In fact, with some of the groups, the name is better than the music!

GOOD SPORTS

Where are the biggest zoos? Not in parks.

They're probably in our stadiums and arenas. And not just when the fans act crazy, either.

Think of it. How many millions of people go out to Detroit to see the Tigers, or to Toronto to see the Blue Jays, or to Baltimore to see the Orioles? And that's just in the American (baseball) League.

The National League has its share, too, with the St. Louis Cardinals and Chicago Cubs.

The story is the same in football. Think of the Colts in Baltimore, the Bears in Chicago, the Bengals in Cincinnati, the Broncos in Denver, the Lions in Detroit, the Rams in Los Angeles, the Dolphins in Miami, the Eagles in Philadelphia, the Chargers in San Diego, and the Seahawks in Seattle. National Football League boss Pete Rozelle may be the country's No. 1 zoo-keeper.

Basketball has plenty of giants, but just a few animal-name teams: the Chicago Bulls and the Milwaukee Bucks.

In the National Hockey League, however, you'll find Bruins in Boston, Red Wings in Detroit, and Penguins in Pittsburgh.

But the best nicknames belong to the college teams. There are Tigers — at Princeton, Auburn, Grambling, Jackson State, Memphis State, Missouri, University of Pacific, Tennessee State, Texas Southern, Doane, and Wittenberg, among others.

Lions? Sure. Columbia has them. And Penn State has Nittany Lions. (Why Nittany? Penn State is located in the Nittany Valley, that's why.)

What about Wildcats? Plenty of them — at Arizona, Davidson, Kentucky, Kansas State,

New Hampshire, Northwestern, Weber State, and Chico State.

If you're a Bulldog fan, you have to root for The Citadel, Drake, Fresno State, Georgia, Louisiana Tech, Mississippi State, South Carolina State, and Yale.

There are all sorts of bears. The Baylor Bears. The Brown Bears. The California Golden Bears. The Cincinnati Bearcats. The Maine Black Bears. The UCLA Bruins. And the Montana Grizzlies.

Some teams really fly high. For instance, the Tennessee Tech Golden Eagles, the Temple Owls, and the Rice Owls, South Carolina's Fighting Gamecocks, Oregon's Ducks, Boston College's Eagles, Kansas's Jayhawks, Illinois State's Redbirds, Air Force's Falcons, and St. Joseph's Hawks.

Among the more unusual team pets: Arkansas's Razorback (a hog), Maryland's Terrapin (turtle), Michigan's Wolverine, Minnesota's Golden Gopher, TCU's Horned Frog, and Southern Illinois' Saluki (a dog).

And, if by the end of the season you haven't been destroyed by North Carolina State's Wolfpack, stung by Delaware State's Hornets, or stampeded by West Texas State's Buffaloes, you can sit down to a fine post-season meal with Virginia Tech's clucking Gobbler.

WHAT'S IN A NAME?

The Chinese take the animal name game to its limits. They name each year after their favorite animal friends.

Take 1980, for instance. To the Chinese, it's the Year of the Monkey. Then come the Year of the Rooster (1981), the Year of the Dog (1982), and the Year of the (oink-oink) Pig (1983).

Other Chinese years include the Rat, the Ox, the Tiger, the Hare (or Rabbit), the Dragon, the Snake, the Horse, and the Sheep (or Goat).

Of course, the Chinese year differs from the calendar most people use. It consists of 12 months of 29 or 30 days. Every so often they add a leap *month* to catch up with the sun.

Practice Shelf-Hypnosis!

Cast a bright spell over your bookshelves and
turn your book collection from dull to Dynamite!
Collect the complete set of Dynamite Books:

Magic Wanda's Dynamite Magic Book
Count Morbida's Dynamite Puzzle Book
The Dynamite Party Book
The Dynamite Book of Top Secret Information
The Dynamite Monster Hall of Fame
The Dynamite Book of Bummers
The Officially Official Dynamite Club Handbook
The Dynamite Year-Round Catalog of Hot Stuff
The Dynamite People Book
Count Morbida's Fang-tastic Activity Book
A Laugh and a Half: The Dynamite Book of Funny Stuff
The Dynamite 3-D Poster Book
Good Vibrations: Straight Talk and Solid Advice For Kids
The Dynamite Animal Hall of Fame

Photo Credits: Wide World Photos: 3, 37, 38, 45, 55, 56, 61, 62, 69, 75, 79.
Columbia Pictures Industries: 5, 71. Culver Pictures: 6, 11, 21, 23, 24, 95.
Lassie Productions, Inc.: 8. Paramount Pictures: 12. Mulberry Square Prod-
uctions: 13, 15. Martha Swope: 17. Walt Disney: 28. ABC: 30. Universal
Pictures: 32, 34. UPI: 40, 67, 78, 83, 91. Science Service, Inc.: 42, 81.
Guiding Eyes for the Blind: 49. Marion Bernstein: 59. NBC: 65. Ursula D.
Mahoney: 73. Dick Swift: 77. Leonard Lee Rue III: 85. Three Lions: 86.
Phoenix Zoo Photo: 89.